from SEA TO SHINING SEA

HAWAII

By Dennis Brindell Fradin

CONSULTANT

Robert L. Hillerich, Ph.D., Professor Emeritus, Bowling Green State University;
Consultant, Pinellas County Schools, Florida

CHILDRENS PRESS®
CHICAGO

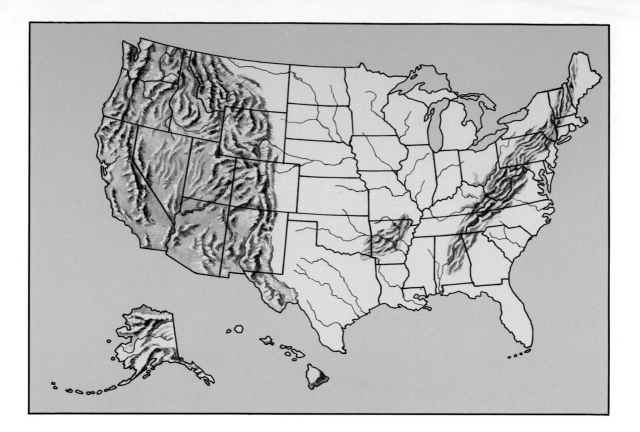

Hawaii is a group of islands in the North Pacific Ocean. It is the only state in the United States that is not a part of the mainland of North America.

For the Ferdinands—Rolene, Alvin, Sonya, and Juliane—with love

Front cover picture: Boats moored in Lahaina Harbor, Maui; page 1: Ka'anapali Beach, Maui; back cover, Opaekaa Falls, Kauai

Project Editor: Joan Downing
Design Director: Karen Kohn
Typesetting: Graphic Connections, Inc.
Engraving: Liberty Photoengraving

8 9 10 11 12 13 R 02 01

Library of Congress Cataloging-in-Publication Data

Fradin, Dennis B.
  Hawaii / by Dennis Brindell Fradin.
    p.   cm. — (From sea to shining sea)
  Includes index.
  ISBN 0-516-03811-7
  1. Hawaii—Juvenile literature. [I. Hawaii.] I. Title.
II. Series: Fradin, Dennis B. From sea to shining sea.
DU623.25.F23   1994b   93-42560
996.9—dc20   CIP
                                                      AC

Table of Contents

Children at the Kamehameha festivities on the island of Kauai

Introducing the Aloha State

Hawaii is the only state made up entirely of islands. It is also the only state that is not in North America. Hawaii lies in the Pacific Ocean.

Hawaii is called the "Aloha State." *Aloha* is a Hawaiian word meaning "love." Hawaiians say aloha instead of hello and good-bye.

Hawaii is a colorful state. Fiery volcanoes tower over white and black sand beaches. Deep-green plants and trees shade blue streams and waterfalls.

Millions of visitors enjoy the state's warmth and beauty each year. They are greeted by having leis placed around their necks. Tourism has become a major business.

Sugarcane and pineapple grow well in Hawaii. Hawaiian factories make sugar, canned pineapple, and pineapple juice.

The Aloha State is special in other ways. What state was completely formed by volcanoes? What is the newest state? What state once had its own kings and queens? Where was children's author Lois

Leis are necklaces made of flowers.

Lowry born? Where was Camp Fire Girls founder Luther Gulick born? The answer to these questions is: Hawaii.

Overleaf: The crater of Haleakala Volcano, Haleakala National Park, Maui

A picture map of Hawaii

A Land Called Paradise

A Land Called Paradise

Cinder cones at Haleakala National Park, Maui

Hawaii is south of the Tropic of Cancer. It is in the mid-Pacific Ocean. Hawaii is the farthest south of any state. On Hawaii Island is Ka Lae, or South Point. That is the southernmost spot in the United States.

Hawaii is a chain of islands. The 132 Hawaiian Islands cover 6,471 square miles. Only three of the other forty-nine states are smaller. Most of the Hawaiian Islands are very small. They aren't even shown on maps. In fact, 124 islands have no people. They are made up of rock, coral, and sand. Those islands cover only 4 square miles.

Eight major islands make up the other 6,467 square miles. They are Hawaii, Maui, Kahoolawe, Lanai, Molokai, Oahu, Kauai, and Niihau. The island of Hawaii is called the "Big Island." All the islands were formed by volcanoes. Today, these volcanoes are the islands' mountains. Mauna Kea is a volcano on the Big Island. It is the state's highest point. Mauna Kea rises 13,796 feet above sea level.

Rich soil lies on Hawaii's plains and valleys. Cattle and sheep graze there. Sugarcane, pineapple, coffee, and nuts grow well on those lands.

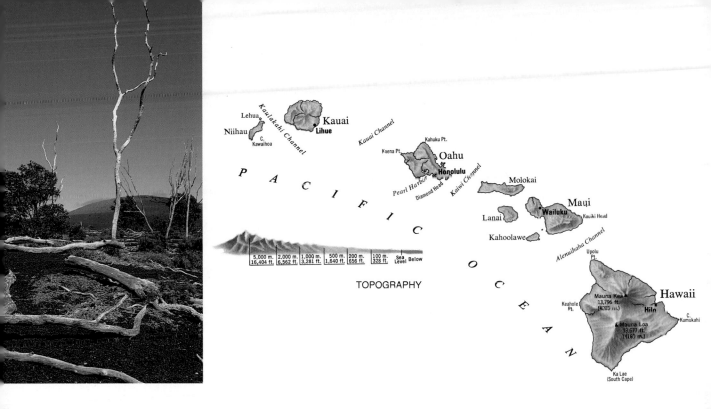

TOPOGRAPHY

The coastline of the eight islands is 1,052 miles long. White sand beaches cover much of the coastline. Black sand made from lava makes up other beaches.

The state has no large rivers or lakes. The Wailuku River on Hawaii is the longest river. Lake Halalii on Niihau is Hawaii's biggest natural lake. Wahiawa Reservoir on Oahu is the state's largest artificially made lake.

CLIMATE

Hawaii is in the tropics. But cool ocean breezes create a heavenly climate. In fact, people sometimes

Left: Devastation Trail, in Hawaii Volcanoes National Park

Below: Kaimu Black Sand Beach, on Hawaii Island

call Hawaii "Paradise." Hawaii has mild temperatures all year. Summer temperatures are about 82 degrees Fahrenheit. Winter temperatures are about 77 degrees Fahrenheit. Parts of Hawaii are dry. They receive less than 10 inches of rain a year. Other areas are very rainy. Mount Waialeale, on Kauai, is the world's wettest place. Rainfall there is about 460 inches a year.

Snow sometimes whitens the state's highest peaks. Many children in Hawaii have never played in snow. Some teachers on Maui drive up Mount

Waimanu Valley, Hamakua Coast, on the island of Hawaii

Haleakala after a snowfall. They bring back snow-balls in ice chests for their students.

PLANTS AND ANIMALS

Hawaii has 2,500 kinds of plants found nowhere else. Other plants are rare elsewhere. The kukui is the state tree. This is also called the candlenut tree. It produces an oil used to make candles and dyes. Hawaii's paper mulberry trees provided cloth for the island's first people. Wood from the monkeypod

Pailoa Bay and a black sand beach in Waianapanapa State Park, Maui

Hawaii is famous for its beautiful orchids (above) and colorful poinsettias (below).

tree is used to make bowls. The autograph tree's leaves are thick enough to write on. Breadfruit trees also grow there. The fruit from these trees tastes a little like bread.

The yellow hibiscus is the state flower. Hawaii is famous for its orchids. Hundreds of different kinds grow there. The poinsettia is a colorful Hawaiian flower. It is popular at Christmastime.

Humpback whales swim off Hawaii's shores. These whales are 50 feet long and have big flippers. The humpback whale is the state mammal. At least seventeen kinds of sharks enter Hawaiian waters. Yet, shark attacks are rare there. The Hawaiian

monk seal is found only in Hawaii. The world's largest sea turtles are also found along the coast. Leatherback turtles weigh up to 1,500 pounds.

Mongooses scoot about Hawaii. They eat rats. Geckos are common in Hawaii. These little lizards are supposed to bring good luck. Wild sheep, wild goats, and Hawaiian bats also live in the state.

The *nene*, or Hawaiian goose, is the state bird. The *oo* is a rare bird. It lives only in Hawaii. Ancient Hawaiians thought its call sounded like "OH-oh." The *io*, or Hawaiian hawk, first lived in Hawaii. The albatross is a common Hawaiian seabird. It is known for its crash landings.

The Hawaiian green sea turtle (above) and Hawaiian monk seal (below) are endangered species.

From Ancient Times
Until Today

From Ancient Times Until Today

Hundreds of millions of years ago, there were no Hawaiian Islands. About 30 million years ago, cracks started to open in the ocean floor. The cracks were volcanoes. Lava poured out of them. This hot liquid hardened. It formed underwater volcanic mountains. As lava kept erupting, the mountains grew. They rose out of the water. These mountains became the Hawaiian Islands.

Over time, rocky lava on the islands crumbled. It turned into soil. Birds, wind, and ocean waters dropped seeds on the islands. They took root. Plants began to grow. But thousands of years would pass before people lived in Hawaii.

The First Hawaiians

The first Hawaiians were Polynesians. They came from western Pacific Islands. The first Polynesians came to Hawaii from the Marquesas Islands. That was about 2,000 years ago. These people were very short. About 800 years later, other Polynesians came from Tahiti. They were very tall. They traveled

Opposite: Early Polynesians traveled to Hawaii in huge double canoes.

Hawaii is the only state formed completely by volcanoes.

Ancient petroglyphs (rock carvings) in South Kohala, on the Big Island

Hawaiian Village at the Polynesian Cultural Center on the island of Oahu

in huge double canoes. The canoes' sails were made from coconut fibers. The Polynesians brought sugarcane, bananas, chickens, dogs, and pigs with them.

The Polynesians named the largest island Hawaii. The whole chain of islands was also named Hawaii. The name is believed to have honored Hawaii Loa. He was the chief said to have led people to the islands. Or, perhaps, the name honored Havaiki. This was an island from which some early Hawaiians had come.

The early Hawaiians built homes of grass and branches. They fished in the ocean with nets and hooks. One of their main foods was *poi*. This was made by cooking taro plant stems. Then the stems were pounded into paste. Women pounded paper mulberry tree bark into tapa. This is a soft cloth. They used the tapa to make clothing.

The Hawaiians believed in many spirits and gods. To them, clouds were spirits of the dead. Pele was the volcano goddess. She lived inside active volcanoes. When she became angry, she would stamp her foot. The volcano would then erupt.

The early Hawaiians often fought among themselves. They followed rules called *kapus*. That meant forbidden things. It was kapu for women and men

Hawaiians call hardened lava that looks like hair "Pele's hair." Lava that hardened like water drops is called "Pele's tears."

to eat together. A common person's shadow falling upon a chief was also kapu. Punishment for breaking some kapus was death.

Captain James Cook (below) brought his ships to Kealakekua Bay (above) on the island of Hawaii.

EUROPEANS ARRIVE

Explorers from Spain, the Netherlands, and Japan may have reached Hawaii about 1550. Juan Gaetano was a Spanish explorer. He drew a map of the Hawaiian Islands in 1555. Little else is known of these voyages.

James Cook, an English explorer, arrived in 1778. His ships the *Resolution* and the *Discovery* landed at Kauai that January. The Hawaiians brought food and water to Cook and his 145 men.

king of Hawaiian crops. Chinese, Japanese, and Polynesian people came to work on the sugar plantations. Most of the sugar was shipped to the United States.

In 1840, the Hawaiians wrote a constitution. They began electing some officials. King Kamehameha III gave many rights to his people. By 1843, Hawaii was recognized as an independent country.

David Kalakaua (1836-1891) was elected king in 1874. The "Merry Monarch" revived the hula and other Hawaiian customs. He also was forced to accept a new constitution. In it, the *haoles* were given much power. *Haole* is a Hawaiian word meaning "white-skinned foreigner."

Over the years, foreigners had brought many diseases to Hawaii. Thousands of Hawaiians died. By 1880, only 50,000 native Hawaiians remained.

THE REPUBLIC OF HAWAII

King Kalakaua died in 1891. Liliuokalani, his sister, then became Hawaii's ruler. She tried to put native Hawaiians in the government. But many Americans and Europeans wanted to take charge of Hawaii. They saw it as a stepping-stone for controlling the

King Kalakaua

Pacific. In 1893, American businessmen overthrew Queen Liliuokalani. United States troops helped them. The Kingdom of Hawaii ended.

The Republic of Hawaii (1894-1898) took its place. Americans ran the country. Sanford B. Dole became the republic's president. He had been born in Hawaii. But his parents were Americans.

Hawaii's American sugar planters wanted the United States to own Hawaii. They would then make more money selling sugar to the United States. The United States government took control of Hawaii in 1898.

Members of the cabinet of the Republic of Hawaii posed for this picture at their last meeting. President Sanford B. Dole is in the center.

Sanford B. Dole was inaugurated governor of the Territory of Hawaii on June 14, 1900.

Native Hawaiians are the descendants of the Polynesians who first came to Hawaii.

THE TERRITORY OF HAWAII

In 1900, Hawaii was made a United States territory. All native Hawaiians became American citizens. But native Hawaiians lost power during territorial times. The best jobs and government offices went to the haoles. Hawaii became more like the United States mainland. Telephones were installed. Hotels were built. The islands became a vacationland. The University of Hawaii was founded in 1907. The next year the United States began a navy base. It was built at Pearl Harbor on Oahu Island.

Pineapple plants had been brought to Hawaii in 1885. In the early 1900s, pineapple became a big crop. People from the Philippines came to help grow pineapple and sugar. Koreans and Puerto Ricans joined them. By 1910, the population had climbed back to nearly 200,000.

In 1917, the United States entered World War I (1914-1918). Nearly 10,000 Hawaiians helped the United States win that war. The Hawaiians then felt that they deserved statehood. But the United States Congress turned them down.

Until 1927, visiting Hawaii meant a long trip by ship. In that year, two army officers made the first mainland-to-Hawaii flight. A. F. Hegenberger and L. J. Maitland arrived from California in the *Bird of Paradise*. Soon airlines were bringing visitors to Hawaii.

The Great Depression (1929-1939) was a time of hardship for Americans. The hard times hurt Hawaii's pineapple and sugar industries. Many farm workers lost their jobs. People could not afford vacations. They stopped coming to Hawaii. Franklin D. Roosevelt went to the islands in 1934. He was the first United States president to visit Hawaii.

The coming of World War II (1939-1945) helped end the depression. For two years, the

These members of the Aloha Brigade were on their way to fight in World War I in 1917.

United States stayed out of the war. Then, on December 7, 1941, Japanese planes attacked. They rained bombs on Pearl Harbor and Hickam Air Field. Within a few hours, 8 ships were sunk and 188 aircraft were destroyed. Nearly 2,500 American sailors, soldiers, and marines were killed. About half of them were aboard the battleship *Arizona*.

The next day, the United States entered the war. Hawaii became the supply and training center for the United States Pacific forces. More than 400,000 Americans in service were stationed in Hawaii.

Japanese Americans were treated badly during the war. United States lawmakers feared they would help Japan. About 110,000 Japanese Americans on

Right: The Japanese bombing ships in Pearl Harbor
Left: These Japanese American soldiers were honored in 1942 at Iolani Palace.

the mainland were sent to special camps. About 1,500 Japanese Americans in Hawaii were sent to Sand Island. But there was no reason to doubt their loyalty. Japanese Americans fought bravely for the United States. Hawaiians of Japanese background served in the 442nd Regiment. They also helped win the war in the 100th Battalion. These were two of the most-decorated United States groups of the war.

A few years later, the United States entered the Korean War (1950-1953). Japanese Americans and Korean Americans from Hawaii helped the United States. About 350 Hawaiians gave their lives.

THE FIFTIETH STATE

Other territories had become states when they had 60,000 people. By 1959, Hawaii had more than 600,000 people. On August 21 of that year, Hawaii became the fiftieth state. The United States then adopted the fifty-star flag.

For many years, Hawaii's main businesses centered around sugar and pineapple. But between 1955 and 1990, Hawaii's pineapple output was sliced in half. Growers found workers in other countries. They worked for less money than did

Hawaii became the fiftieth state on August 21, 1959. Alaska had become the forty-ninth state on January 3 of that year.

25

Waikiki Beach

Renaissance *means "rebirth."*

Hawaiians. Lanai Island is owned by the Dole Company. It was once the world's pineapple capital. Dole closed its Lanai cannery in 1992. In 1992, Hawaiians cut one-third less sugarcane than they did in 1987.

But during these years, tourism grew. Faster planes began flying to Hawaii in 1959. More vacationers arrived. Dozens of new hotels were built. Former pineapple and sugar workers found jobs serving tourists. By 1972, 2 million people were visiting Hawaii each year. That figure was nearly 7 million by 1991. Some visitors liked Hawaii so much that they moved there. Between 1960 and 1990, Hawaii's population almost doubled to 1,115,274.

Hawaii has much to be proud about. In 1974, the state government ordered employers to offer health insurance to workers. It became the first state to do that. Hawaii did so through its Prepaid Health Care Act. In 1993, a plan like Hawaii's was suggested for the whole country. By 1993, Hawaii had one of the country's lowest jobless rates.

The "Hawaiian Renaissance" began in the 1970s. Interest in native Hawaiian music, dance, and language was reborn. By 1991, the public schools had begun a special program. Through it, children were taught in the Hawaiian language.

Recently, native Hawaiians have been fighting for land. In 1921, the United States government granted land to them. But thousands never received it. Many native Hawaiians have lived in poverty since 1898. Receiving the promised land would improve their way of life.

In 1999, Hawaii will celebrate its fortieth birthday as a state. By then, perhaps, the native Hawaiians will have won their struggle. To be a true paradise, all Hawaiians must have a good life.

Dancers performing at the Polynesian Cultural Center

Overleaf: Hawaiian women in muumuus at the Polynesian Cultural Center

Hawaiians and Their Work

HAWAIIANS AND THEIR WORK

Hawaii's population is about 1.1 million. Only ten states have fewer people. Many different kinds of people live in Hawaii. The state has been called "A Rainbow of Peoples."

Hawaii is proud of having people of many backgrounds. This was shown in its first state lawmakers. William F. Quinn became the state's first governor. He was white. Hiram Fong was a Chinese American. He was one of Hawaii's first two United States senators. Daniel Inouye was a Japanese American. He was Hawaii's first member in the United States House of Representatives. James Kealoha became lieutenant governor. He had Polynesian ancestors.

About 6 out of 10 Hawaiians have Asian or Pacific Island backgrounds. These people make up the largest group of Hawaiians. One-fourth of the state's people are Japanese Americans. One-fifth are native Hawaiians. One-tenth have roots in the Philippines. And 1 in 20 is Chinese American.

One-third of the state's people are white. Their ancestors came from Germany, England, and the

Hawaii is the only state in which white people are not the largest group.

29

United States. More than 80,000 Hawaiians are Hispanic. Their ancestors came mostly from Spain and Puerto Rico. Nearly 30,000 Hawaiians are black. Another 5,000 are American Indians.

THEIR WORK

Over half of all Hawaiians have jobs. Selling goods is the state's most popular kind of work. About one-fourth of Hawaii's 550,000 workers do this.

Another one-fourth of Hawaiian workers provide services. They include repair people, lawyers, and nurses. Hawaii has many doctors for a state its size. They do a good job. Hawaiians live to be about seventy-seven years old. That is the longest life span in the country.

Over 100,000 Hawaiians work for the government. Thousands of them are in the military. Many are stationed at Pearl Harbor Naval Base. Others are at Kaneohe Bay Marine Corps Air Station. Public-school teachers are among the other government workers. They, too, do a good job. Five of every six Hawaiians finish high school. That is one of the country's highest graduation rates.

About 15,000 Hawaiians farm. Hawaii is a leader at growing sugarcane. Papayas, guavas, mangoes,

A park ranger at Hawaii Volcanoes National Park

and coconuts are grown in Hawaii. They are called tropical fruits. Other farm crops include pineapples, bananas, grapefruit, oranges, macadamia nuts, and orchids. Beef cattle, eggs, and milk are other farm products. Hawaii is the only state that grows coffee. It is famous for Kona coffee. That grows on the Big Island's Kona Coast.

More than 21,000 Hawaiians make goods. Foods are the top product. Hawaii ranks high at making sugar and pineapple products. Taro chips and guava and papaya jams and jellies are other foods from Hawaii. Brightly colored "aloha shirts" and other clothing are made in Hawaii. Chemicals are made there, too. They include a medicine for cancer.

A pineapple harvest on the Dole plantation

Hawaii produces more than 1 billion pounds of cane sugar a year. That is 4 pounds for each person in the United States.

Overleaf: An aerial view of Honolulu and Diamond Head at dusk

31

A Trip Through the Aloha State

A Trip Through the Aloha State

awaii is like no other state. The Aloha State's beautiful land and warm weather attract many visitors. They can enjoy native Hawaiian food and music. Visitors go from island to island by boat or plane. This is called island hopping.

Oahu: The Gathering Place

Oahu *means "gathering place."*

The "Gathering Place" is a fitting nickname for Oahu Island. Three-fourths of the state's people live there. Oahu has nine of the state's ten largest cities. Honolulu is on Oahu. That is the state's capital and largest city. About 365,000 people live there. That is ten times more people than Hawaii's next-largest city.

Visitors may watch lawmakers working at the state capitol in Honolulu. No other state has a capitol like it. The Senate and House of Representatives chambers are cone-shaped. They look like volcanoes.

Honolulu has the only royal palaces in the United States. King Kalakaua built Iolani Palace.

The capitol, in Honolulu

His throne and that of Queen Liliuokalani are there. *Iolani Palace*
Outside of Honolulu is the Queen Emma Summer
Palace. Queen Emma and her husband, King
Kamehameha IV, spent summers there.

Long ago, Hawaiian chiefs wore long cloaks.
They were made from thousands of bird feathers.
These feathered garments are displayed at
Honolulu's Bishop Museum. This is Hawaii's
largest museum. Old Hawaiian canoes and jewelry
can also be seen there.

Waikiki Beach is in east Honolulu. Hotels line
this famous 2-mile strip of sand. In the evening,
hotels host *luaus*. At luaus, guests eat roast pig and
poi. Some of them learn how to hula.

Nearby is Diamond Head. This is a 760-foot-tall volcano. People once mistook its volcanic glass for diamonds.

West of Honolulu is Pearl Harbor. The *Arizona* Memorial is there. The battleship lies underwater where it was sunk on December 7, 1941. The memorial building floats atop the ship. Navy boats take visitors out to the memorial.

North of Pearl Harbor is Waipahu. It is the state's fifth-largest city. Plantation Village is there. It shows what life was like on an early Hawaiian sugar plantation.

Nuuanu Pali is a few miles north of Honolulu. This 1,200-foot cliff offers a beautiful view. Its

The U.S.S. Arizona
National Memorial

name means "bone-chilling cliff." In 1795, 500 warriors died there. Kamehameha the Great's forces drove them over the cliff.

The Byodo-In Temple

Kailua is to the north. It is Hawaii's third-biggest city. Ula Po Heiau is an ancient Hawaiian temple. It is in Kailua. Visitors to Kailua Beach can take windsurfing lessons. Kaneohe is to the west. It is the fourth-largest Hawaiian city. The Byodo In Temple is a Kaneohe landmark. It looks like a 900-year-old building in Japan.

The Polynesian Cultural Center is near Laie in northern Oahu. There, villages from seven South Pacific islands have been rebuilt. People from those islands show how Polynesian crafts and clothing are

Nuuanu Pali

made. In the evening, Polynesian music and dances are performed.

KAUAI AND NIIHAU ISLANDS

Kauai is northwest of Oahu. This island has green valleys, waterfalls, and beautiful flowers. The flowers gave Kauai its nickname: the "Garden Island."

Wailua Falls is at Kauai's east end. It is made of two falls. They drop 80 feet from a cliff. Not far away is the Sleeping Giant. This mountain ridge looks like a large person lying down.

To the south is Lihue. This is Kauai's main city. Close to Lihue is the Menehune Fish Pond. The pond's wall is 900 feet long and 5 feet high. The Menehunes were said to have built it in one night. The Menehunes were probably the people who came from the Marquesas Islands. Menehune Ditch is also on Kauai. The Menehunes built it to bring water to their fields.

The Hawaiian Islands have many lava tubes. Flowing lava created these tunnels. A lava tube in which ocean waves spout upward is called a blowhole. The Spouting Horn is a blowhole. It is at Kauai's southern tip. The Spouting Horn is also known for its strange moaning noises.

Wailua *means "twin waters."*

A lava tube at Hawaii Volcanoes National Park

The colorful Waimea Canyon is on western Kauai. The Waimea River carved this half-mile-deep canyon. Its stone walls are red, blue, gold, and green. Barking Sands Beach is nearby. The sand there gets very dry. When walked on, it makes a "woof-woof" sound.

Southwest of Kauai is Niihau Island. It is called the "Forbidden Island." Visitors must receive an invitation from its owners. In 1864, Elizabeth Sinclair bought the island from King Kamehameha V. Her descendants, the Robinson family, own it today.

The island's 250 people are descendants of Hawaii's first Polynesians. Most of them work on

Bougainvillea blooms on Kauai

the Robinson cattle ranch. Cars and televisions are not allowed. The island's children learn Hawaiian as well as English.

MOLOKAI, LANAI, AND KAHOOLAWE

Molokai, Lanai, and Kahoolawe are east of Oahu. Molokai's northeast coast has the world's highest-known sea cliffs. They tower 3,300 feet above the ocean. There are only about 7,000 people on Molokai. It is called the "Friendly Island."

On the island's north side is Kalaupapa Peninsula. In the 1860s, Hawaiians with leprosy were sent there. This disease killed thousands of Hawaiians. In 1873, Father Damien (Joseph de Veuster) arrived from Belgium. This priest cared for the leprosy patients. He helped them build homes and grow crops. In 1889, Father Damien died from the disease. The place where he worked is now Kalaupapa National Historical Park.

Lanai is south of Molokai. It is called the "Pineapple Island." Some call it the "Private Island." The Dole Company owns the island. Until 1992, Dole grew huge amounts of pineapple there. Now Dole's owners are building large hotels on Lanai.

Father Damien with some leprosy patients on Molokai. Since Father Damien's time, medicines have been found that cure leprosy.

Garden of the Gods is in northwest Lanai. The land there looks much like the moon's surface. Large rocks in the garden were formed by lava. They are colorful and have strange shapes. Luahiwa Petroglyphs are in the middle of Lanai. These are pictures carved long ago in rocks. One carving there shows a big canoe. It may be a picture of the first Polynesians' journey to Hawaii.

Garden of the Gods

Kahoolawe is south of Lanai. It is called the "Uninhabited Island." Kahoolawe was a sacred place to early Hawaiians. They considered the island the center of the universe. Many of the island's ancient temples still stand. But no one has lived on

41

The harbor at Lahaina, Maui, with mountains rising in the background

Kahoolawe for many years. Since 1941, the United States navy has used Kahoolawe as a bombing target. Some Native Hawaiians want to gain control of the island again.

MAUI: THE VALLEY ISLAND

Maui is the second-biggest of the Hawaiian Islands. It was named for an ancient superhero called Maui. Rugged mountains rise on Maui. The mountain valleys gave Maui its nickname, the "Valley Island."

Mount Haleakala is a volcano. It is in east Maui. The volcano is part of Haleakala National Park.

Haleakala means "house of the sun." Maui, the hero, was said to have slowed down the sun. That way people could have more daylight. Today, visitors enjoy watching the sun rise from the volcano's rim. The Seven Pools of Kipahulu are also part of the park. Waterfalls form seven large pools. Visitors enjoy swimming in their cool water.

Humpback whales spend their winters in Maalaea Bay. That is off southwest Maui. McGregor Point overlooks the bay. It is a good place to see adult and baby humpbacks.

Hawaii: The Big Island

The island of Hawaii is the largest of the Hawaiian Islands. The state of Hawaii's second-largest city is Hilo. It is on the east side of the Big Island. Hilo has nearly 40,000 people. The Lyman House and Museum is in Hilo. American missionaries built the house in 1839. The museum has Hawaiian wood carvings and Polynesian clothing. Each spring, the Merry Monarch Hula Festival is held in Hilo. Included is a three-day hula competition. Hawaiians say that Pele's sister danced the first hula. She did it to honor her sister. Today, the hula is part of many Hawaiian gatherings.

Sunrise at the Seven Pools of Kipahulu

The Big Island is twice the size of the state of Delaware.

One of the highest waterfalls in the United States is north of Hilo. Akaka Falls drops 442 feet. Rainbow Falls is just west of downtown Hilo. In the early morning, visitors may see a rainbow through the mist of the falls.

Kalapana Black Sand Beach is along the Big Island's southeast coast. It was formed when hot lava hit the cooler ocean water. The lava broke apart and hardened into tiny grains.

Hawaii Volcanoes National Park is also on the southeast side of the Big Island. Mauna Loa, the world's biggest volcano, is there. Its last eruption was in 1985. Kilauea is also in the park. It is nick-named the "Drive-in Volcano." Visitors can walk

Lava and a steam cloud at Kilauea, Hawaii Volcanoes National Park

from their cars to watch the bubbling lava. The
Hawaiian Volcano Observatory is at Kilauea. There
scientists study the volcano's movement.

Cowboys herding cattle on the Parker Ranch

On the northwest part of the Big Island is
Parker Ranch. John Parker started the ranch in
1847. Today, it is one of the country's biggest sin-
gle-owner ranches. Parker Ranch covers 350 square
miles. Nearby is the town of Waimea. It was founded by Parker. A museum in Waimea tells the history
of the ranch.

The Captain Cook Monument is on the island's
west side. It is near the spot where Cook was killed
in 1779.

A Gallery of Famous Hawaiians

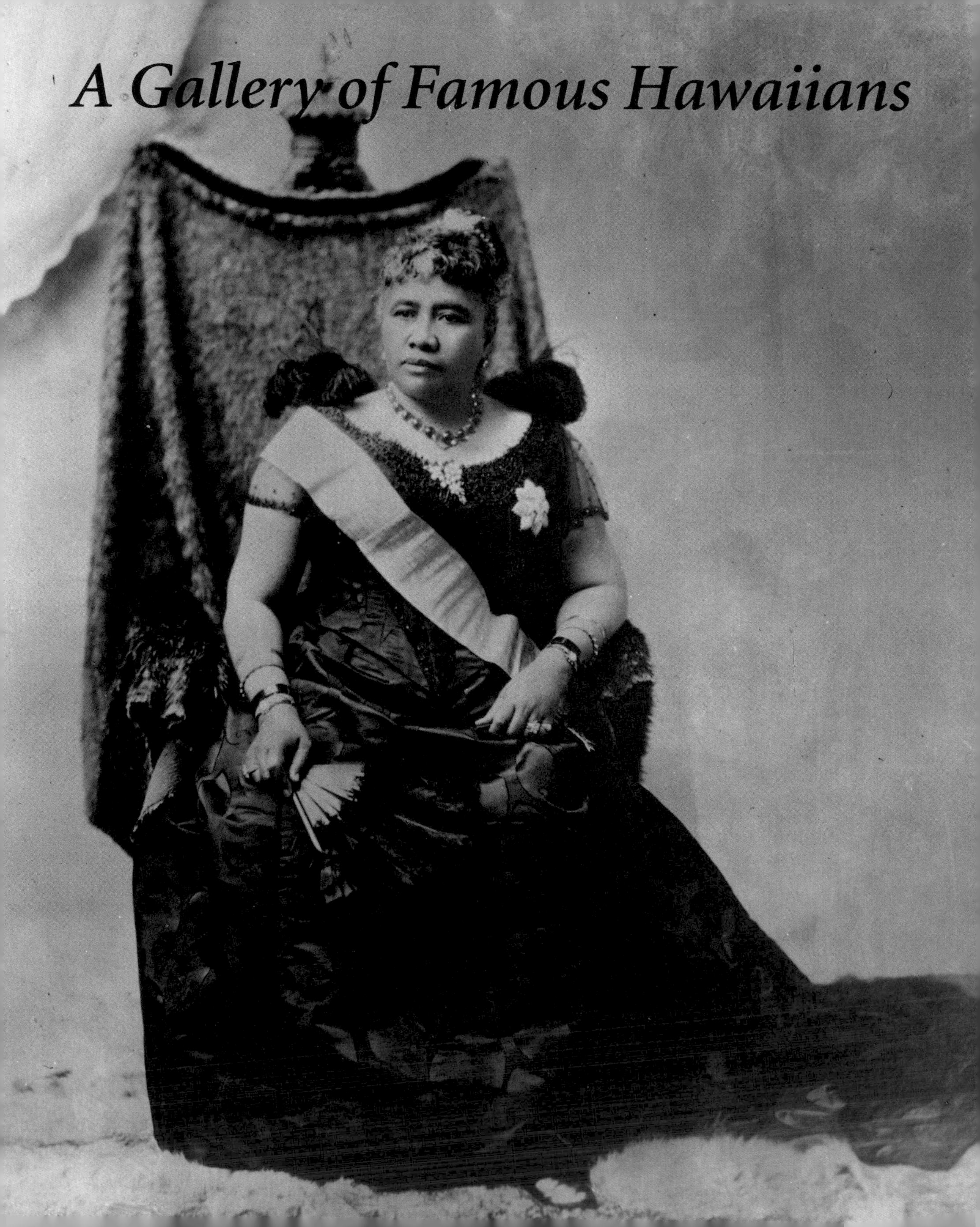

A Gallery of Famous Hawaiians

Hawaii has produced many interesting people. They range from kings and queens to authors and an astronaut. **Kamehameha the Great** (1750?-1819) was born on the Big Island. At 6 feet, 6 inches tall, he was a large man. As a young man, Kamehameha moved the 5,000-pound Naha Stone. Hawaiians believed that whoever could move that stone would rule all the islands. By 1810, Kamehameha had united the islands.

Lydia Liliuokalani (1838-1917) was born in Honolulu. She was queen for two years (1891-1893). Foreign businessmen took over Hawaii's government in 1893. Liliuokalani was imprisoned in Iolani Palace for nearly a year. Today, she is remembered for her many talents. Queen Liliuokalani wrote songs. One of them is the love song "Aloha Oe" ("My Love"). Liliuokalani died at her Honolulu home. It was called Washington Place. Washington Place is now the Hawaii governor's mansion.

Princess Bernice Pauahi Bishop (1838-1884) was born in Honolulu. She was a great-granddaugh-

Opposite: Queen Liliuokalani
Below: Princess Bernice Pauahi Bishop

In her youth, Princess Bernice was engaged to marry Kamehameha V. But she fell in love with American Charles Bishop.

Sarah Pierce Emerson

ter of Kamehameha the Great. The princess was married to **Charles Reed Bishop** (1822-1915). He founded Hawaii's first bank. In 1872, King Kamehameha V was dying. He asked the princess to be Hawaii's next ruler. She refused the offer. Princess Bernice founded the Kamehameha Schools. They are for young native Hawaiians. She also collected Hawaiian relics. They can be seen in Honolulu's Bishop Museum. Charles Bishop founded the museum to honor his wife.

Hiram Bingham (1789-1869) was born in Vermont. He became a minister. In 1820, Bingham led the first American missionaries to Hawaii. He spread Christianity there. Bingham also helped create a written alphabet for the Hawaiian language. Bibles and other books were printed in Hawaiian. By 1850, Hawaiians were among the world's best readers.

Dr. Sarah Pierce Emerson (1855-1938) was from Massachusetts. She moved to Hawaii as a child. Then she moved back to the mainland to study medicine. In 1882, she returned and became one of the first women doctors in Hawaii.

Luther Gulick (1865-1918) was born in Honolulu. He was the son of an American missionary. Gulick also went to the mainland to study. He spent the rest of his life working with young people. At the YMCA in Springfield, Massachusetts, he helped invent basketball (1891). In 1910, he and his wife, **Charlotte Gulick,** founded the Camp Fire Girls. Later, the group became the Camp Fire Boys and Girls.

YMCA stands for Young Men's Christian Association.

Alexander Cartwright (1820-1892) was born in New York City. There he founded one of the country's first baseball teams. Cartwright also wrote baseball's basic rules. In the 1850s, Cartwright moved to Honolulu. He built Hawaii's first baseball field. Hawaiians played baseball before it was known in many states.

Cartwright also helped found Honolulu's fire department.

Pitchers **Ron Darling** and **Sid Fernandez** were born in Honolulu. Darling was born in 1960;

Pitcher Sid Fernandez

Hiram Fong (second from left) was the first Chinese American in the U. S. Senate.

Fernandez, in 1962. Both helped the New York Mets win the 1986 World Series. Fernandez likes to wear uniform number 50. It shows that he is from the fiftieth state.

Duke Paoa Kahanamoku (1889-1968) was born on Maui. Kahanamoku was a great swimmer. In 1912 and 1920, he won Olympic gold medals in swimming. He was also a famous Hawaiian surfer. Surfing was invented long ago by Hawaiians.

Chad Rowan was born in Honolulu in 1969. He grew to be 6 feet 8 inches tall. He weighs about 470 pounds. Rowan became a sumo wrestler. This is a Japanese style of wrestling. It pits huge men against each other. Rowan took the name **Akebono**. In 1993, he became the sumo grand champion. He is the first non-Japanese person to hold that title.

Yau Fong was born in Honolulu in 1907. He greatly admired Hiram Bingham. Fong changed his first name to Hiram. He became a lawyer and entered politics. **Hiram Fong** became one of Hawaii's first two U.S. senators (1959-1977). He was the first Chinese American in the Senate.

Spark Matsunaga

Spark Matsunaga (1916-1990) was born on Kauai. He was a Japanese American. After the Pearl Harbor attack, Matsunaga was imprisoned. When he was freed, he joined the famous 100th/442nd forces. Matsunaga was wounded twice fighting for the United States. Later, he served in the U.S. House of Representatives (1963-1977) and Senate (1977-1990). He helped pass an important law in 1988. It gave an apology and money to Japanese Americans imprisoned during World War II.

Daniel Inouye was born in Honolulu in 1924. While fighting with the 100th/442nd forces, he lost his right arm. Inouye gave up his hope of becoming a doctor. Instead, he became a politician. Inouye served Hawaii in the U.S. House of Representatives (1959-1963). He was the first Japanese American in Congress. He has been a U.S. senator since 1963.

George Ariyoshi was born in Honolulu in 1926. He became a lawyer. Then Ariyoshi was elect-

The 100th Battalion and the 442nd Regiment were combined as the 100th/442nd Regiment.

Oren Long was Hawaii's other senator at this time.

ed Hawaii's governor (1974-1986). He was the first Japanese American governor in the United States.

Patsy Mink was born in 1927 on Maui. She decided that "the highest achievement is to serve other people." Mink worked to help handicapped people. She has also served Hawaii in the U.S. House of Representatives (1965-1977, 1990-present). There, she has worked to improve U.S. schools. She also tries to help the poor.

Three popular entertainers were born in Honolulu. **Clarissa Haili** (1901-1979) became a teacher. Later, this native Hawaiian woman won fame as a singer and dancer. Using the name **Hilo Hattie,** she danced the hula in a comical way. **Don Ho** was born in 1930. Millions of people have heard him sing "Tiny Bubbles." **Bette Midler** was born in 1945. She won a prize for singing "Silent Night" in first grade. Midler became a famous singer and actress.

Ellison S. Onizuka (1946-1986) was born in Kealakekua on the Big Island. He became Hawaii's first astronaut. Ellison's first space flight was in 1985. In 1986, he and six others were killed aboard the space shuttle *Challenger*. In 1991, the Astronaut Ellison S. Onizuka Space Center opened. It is near his birthplace. There, visitors can learn about space.

Bette Midler

Astronaut Ellison S. Onizuka

Lois Lowry was born in Honolulu in 1937. She became a famous children's author. Lowry's Anastasia Krupnik adventures are well known among young people. *The Giver* by Lowry won the 1994 Newbery Medal.

The birthplace of Kamehameha the Great, Ellison S. Onizuka, and Bette Midler...

Home also to Father Damien, Hiram Bingham, Sarah Pierce Emerson, and Alexander Cartwright...

The land of leis, volcanoes, and black sand beaches...

The site of the Pearl Harbor attack, and today a great vacationland...

This is the fiftieth state—Hawaii. Aloha!

Did You Know?

Sea Life Park on Oahu features performing whales and dolphins. In 1985, a new kind of animal was born there. It was called a *wholphin* because its father was a *wha*le and its mother a d*olphin*.

Hula-Hoops were popular in the late 1950s and early 1960s. Children and adults twirled the hoop around their waists by moving like a hula dancer.

Hawaii has a holiday called Lei Day on May 1. There are lei-making contests. Lei Day Queens are chosen.

No one wants to live in a volcano. But 1,500 people live in Volcano—a town on the Big Island.

English explorer James Cook named the Hawaiian Islands the Sandwich Islands. The name honored England's Earl of Sandwich, the same man for whom the sandwich was named. The name stuck to the food, but not to the islands.

The eight stripes on Hawaii's flag represent the state's eight major islands.

Waterfalls usually tumble downward. But Waipuhia Falls on Oahu is nicknamed Upside Down Falls. Strong winds blow its water *up* from the cliff's edge.

Mauna Kea receives enough winter snow for skiing. Yet, on winter days, the mountain is warm enough for people to wear bathing suits while skiing.

Hawaii doesn't have a permanent state fish. Instead, it changes its state fish every few years. Recently, the state fish has been the *humuhumu-nukunukuapuaa.* That means "fish with a nose like a pig's."

The Hawaiian language has just twelve letters— p, k, h, l, m, n, w, a, e, i, o, and u. Some Hawaiian words use the same vowel two or three times in a row. Each vowel is pronounced separately. For instance, *Kaaawa,* a town on Oahu, is pronounced Kah-ah-AH-wah. *Aa,* a kind of lava, is pronounced AH-ah.

Hawaiian Punch is named for the Aloha State. Its many ingredients, such as papaya and guava, are grown there.

The forces that built Hawaii are still at work. A 15,000-foot underwater volcano is 30 miles from the Big Island. When it rises another 3,000 feet, it will poke above the water. This may take 10,000 years. The island has been named *Loihi* ("long") because of its shape.

A Japanese pilot crashed on Niihau Island during World War II. He shot a Hawaiian man three times. The Hawaiian picked up the pilot and threw him against a stone wall. This gave rise to the saying: "Never shoot a Hawaiian more than twice. The third time he gets angry."

Asia's Mount Everest, towering 29,028 feet above sea level, is considered the world's tallest peak. Mauna Kea rises 13,796 feet above sea level. But, if measured down to its base on the ocean floor, Mauna Kea would be the world's tallest peak at 33,500 feet.

Hawaii is the seventh-windiest state. Each spring, contestants show their kite-flying skill at the Oahu Kite Festival.

Hawaii Information

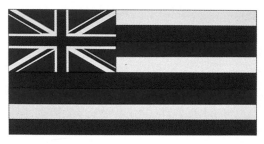

The state flag

Nene (Hawaiian goose)

Area: 6,471 square miles (the forty-seventh largest state)

Length of Hawaiian Island Chain Southeast to Northwest: 1,523 miles

Borders: Mid-Pacific Ocean; the closest state is California, about 2,390 miles away

Highest Point: Mauna Kea on the island of Hawaii, 13,796 feet above sea level

Lowest Point: Sea level, along the coast of all the islands

Hottest Recorded Temperature: 100° F. (at Pahala on the Big Island, on April 27, 1931)

Coldest Recorded Temperature: 12° F. (at Mauna Kea, on May 17, 1979)

Statehood: The fiftieth state, on August 21, 1959

Origin of Name: Named either for Polynesian chief Hawaii Loa, who is believed to have discovered the islands, or for a former island home called *Havaiki*

Capital: Honolulu

Counties: 5

United States Representatives: 2

State Senators: 25

State Representatives: 51

State Song: "Hawaii Ponoi" ("Our Own Hawaii"), by King Kalakaua (words), as a tribute to Kamehameha the Great; and Henry Berger (melody)

State Motto: *Ua mau ke ea o ka aina i ka pono* (coined by King Kamehameha III, meaning "The life of the land is preserved in righteousness")

Nicknames: "Aloha State," "Paradise"

State Seal: Adopted in 1959

State Flag: Adopted in 1959

State Flower: Yellow hibiscus

State Bird: Nene (Hawaiian goose)

State Tree: Kukui (candlenut)

State Mammal: Humpback whale

Major Islands: Hawaii, Oahu, Maui, Lanai, Kauai, Molokai, Kahoolawe, Niihau

Major River: Wailuku River on the island of Hawaii

Major Lakes: Lake Halalii, Wahiawa Reservoir

Some Waterfalls: Akaka Falls, Waikane Falls, Rainbow Falls, Sacred Falls, Wailua Falls

Active Volcanoes: Mauna Loa, Kilauea

Wildlife: Humpback whales, dolphins, seals, sea turtles, geckos and other lizards, wild sheep, wild goats, Hawaiian bats, nenes (Hawaiian geese), albatrosses, Hawaiian hawks, cardinals, mockingbirds, many other kinds of birds, tuna, marlin, bass, sharks, many other kinds of fish

Farm Products: Sugarcane, pineapples, bananas, grapefruit, oranges, beef cattle, hogs, eggs, macadamia nuts, Kona coffee, avocados, mangoes, papayas, guavas, orchids and other flowers, taro

Mining Products: Crushed stone, sand and gravel

Manufactured Products: Processed sugar, canned pineapple, pineapple juice, other foods, "aloha shirts" and other clothing, chemicals, concrete, metal products

Population: 1,108,229, forty-first among the states (1990 U.S. Census Bureau figures)

Major Cities (1990 Census):

Honolulu	365,272	Pearl City	30,993
Hilo	37,808	Waimalu	29,967
Kailua	36,818	Mililani Town	29,359
Kaneohe	35,448	Schofield Barracks	19,597
Waipahu	31,435	Wahiawa	17,386

Yellow hibiscus

Kukui (candlenut) tree

Humpback whale

Hawaii History

About A.D. 100-800—The first Polynesians reach Hawaii

1555—Juan Gaetano, a Spanish explorer, draws maps showing the Hawaiian Islands

1778—English explorer James Cook lands on Kauai

1779—Cook is killed on the island of Hawaii during a return trip to the islands

1789—American ships begin arriving in Hawaii

1795—Kamehameha the Great founds the Kingdom of Hawaii

1819—Kamehameha the Great dies; his son, King Kamehameha II, ends the kapu system

1820—The first American Christian missionaries come to Hawaii

1820s—Hawaii becomes a favorite stop for American whaling ships

1840—Hawaii's first written constitution, setting up an elected legislature, is issued by Kamehameha III

1874—King David Kalakaua, the "Merry Monarch," is elected king, revives customs banned by missionaries, and visits the United States

1882—The Iolani Palace is completed

1891—Liliuokalani becomes queen upon the death of her brother, King Kalakaua

1893—Americans led by Sanford B. Dole overthrow Queen Liliuokalani, ending the Kingdom of Hawaii

1894-98—Hawaii is an independent nation, called the Republic of Hawaii; Sanford B. Dole is the president

1898—The United States gains control of Hawaii

1900—The Territory of Hawaii is established

1901—The Hawaiian Pineapple Company, now the Dole Company is formed

1907—The University of Hawaii is founded

1913—Hawaii's first public library opens in Honolulu

1917-18—Nearly 10,000 Hawaiians serve in World War I

1927—A. F. Hegenberger and L. J. Maitland make the first mainland-to-Hawaii airplane flight

1929-39—During the Great Depression, thousands of people in Hawaii lose their jobs

1934—President Franklin D. Roosevelt becomes the first U.S. president to visit Hawaii

1939—World War II begins

1941-45—On December 7, 1941, the U.S. naval base at Pearl Harbor is attacked by Japanese planes; the United States then enters World War II; Hawaii becomes the center for U.S. Pacific forces; more than 40,000 Hawaiians help win the war

1959—On August 21, Hawaii becomes the fiftieth state

1967—Hawaii attracts 1 million tourists

1969—The state capitol is completed

1974—George Ariyoshi becomes governor of Hawaii, the United States' first governor of Japanese ancestry; Hawaii passes the Prepaid Health Care Act

1982—Eileen Anderson is elected mayor of Honolulu, the first woman mayor in the state

1983—A record 4.4 million visitors spend about $4 billion in Hawaii

1986—John Waihee becomes the Aloha State's first elected governor of Native Hawaiian ancestry

1991—Nearly 7 million people visit the Aloha State

1992—Hurricane Iniki strikes Hawaii, killing three people and causing $1 billion in damages

1994—The U.S. Navy returns control of the island of Kahoolawe to the state of Hawaii

Lester Maitland (left) and Albert Hegenberger made the first airplane flight from the mainland to Hawaii in 1927.

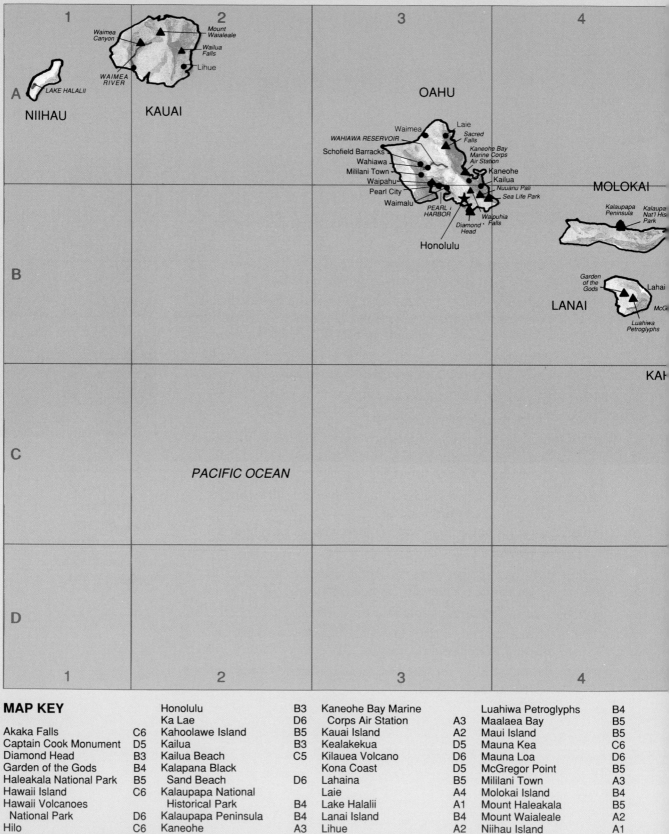

Map labels

1 **2** **3** **4**

KAUAI (grid 2A)
Waimea Canyon
Mount Waialeale
Wailua Falls
Lihue
WAIMEA RIVER
LAKE HALALII

NIIHAU (grid 1A)

OAHU (grid 3A/B)
Waimea
Laie
Sacred Falls
WAHIAWA RESERVOIR
Kaneohe Bay Marine Corps Air Station
Schofield Barracks
Wahiawa
Mililani Town
Waipahu
Kaneohe
Kailua
Nuuanu Pali
Sea Life Park
Pearl City
Waimalu
PEARL HARBOR
Waipuhia Falls
Diamond Head
Honolulu

MOLOKAI (grid 4B)
Kalaupapa Peninsula
Kalaupapa Nat'l His... Park

LANAI (grid 4B)
Garden of the Gods
Lahai...
McG...
Luahiwa Petroglyphs

KAH...

A **B** **C** **D**

PACIFIC OCEAN

1 **2** **3** **4**

MAP KEY

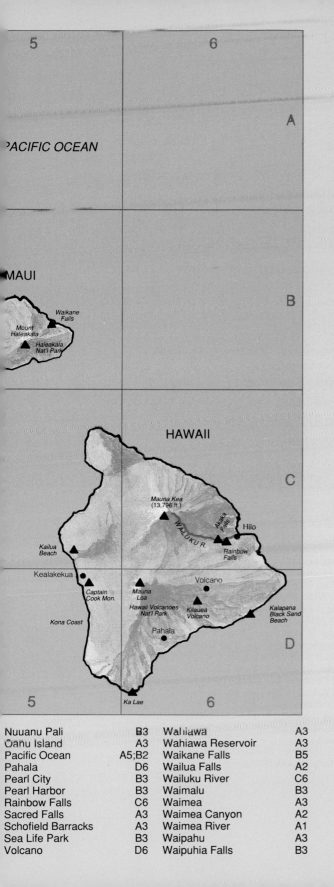

GLOSSARY

ancestor: A person from whom another person is descended, such as a great-grandmother or a great-great-grandfather

ancient: Relating to a time long ago

astronaut: A person highly trained for spaceflight

blowhole: A lava tube through which ocean waves spout

canyon: A deep, steep-sided valley

capital: The city that is the seat of government

capitol: The building in which the government meets

climate: The typical weather of a region

descendant: A person's child or grandchild

explorer: A person who visits and studies unknown lands

lava: Hot liquid from a volcano

lava tube: A tunnel formed by flowing lava

memorial: A structure built in memory of people or an event

million: A thousand thousand (1,000,000)

missionary: A person who leaves home to spread his or her religion in another land

paradise: A wonderful, heavenly place

petroglyph: A picture carved in a rock

plantation: A very large farm

population: The number of people in a place

renaissance: rebirth; the Hawaiian Renaissance is a rebirth of native Hawaiian language, music, and dance

republic: A country with elected officials

sumo: A Japanese style of wrestling

territory: Land owned by a country; with a capital "T," as in Territory of Hawaii, a region with its own government that is owned by a country

tropics: A warm region north and south of the Equator

uninhabited: Having no people

volcano: An opening through which lava and other materials erupt; also, the mountain built by lava

PICTURE ACKNOWLEDGMENTS

Front cover, © Chris Bryant/**Tony Stone Images, Inc.;** 1, © **Tom Till;** 2, **Tom Dunnington;** 3, © David S. Boynton/**Photo Resource Hawaii;** 4-5, **Tom Dunnington;** 6-7, © Buddy Mays/**Travel Stock;** 8, © Kevin Schafer/**Tom Stack & Associates;** 9 (top left), © Steve Vidler/**SuperStock;** 9 (top right), **Courtesy of Hammond, Incorporated, Maplewood, New Jersey;** 9 (bottom), © Clyde H. Smith/**N E Stock Photo;** 10, © Greg Vaughn/**Tom Stack & Associates;** 11, © Larry Ulrich/**Tony Stone Images, Inc.;** 12 (top), © John Elk/**Tony Stone Images, Inc.;** 12 (bottom), © Kohout Productions/**Root Resources;** 13 (top), © Cat and Kevin Sweeney/**Photo Resource Hawaii;** 13 (bottom), © Monte Costa/**Photo Resource Hawaii;** 14, **Bishop Museum, The State Museum of Natural and Cultural History;** 15, © Stephen Graham/**Dembinsky Photo Assoc.;** 16, © **James P. Rowan;** 17 (both pictures), **North Wind Picture Archives, hand colored;** 18, © John Elk/**Tony Stone Images, Inc.;** 19, © **Cameramann International, Ltd.;** 20, **North Wind Picture Archives;** 21, **North Wind Picture Archives;** 22, **North Wind Picture Archives;** 23, **Bishop Museum, The State Museum of Natural and Cultural History;** 24 (both pictures), **AP/Wide World Photos;** 25, **AP/Wide World Photos;** 26, © David Austen/**Tony Stone Images, Inc.;** 27, © **Cameramann International, Ltd.;** 28, © **Cameramann International, Ltd.;** 29 (top), © Joe Carini/**Tony Stone Images, Inc.;** 29 (bottom), © Phil Degginger/**Tony Stone Images, Inc.;** 30, © **Cameramann International, Ltd.;** 31, © **Cameramann International, Ltd.;** 32-33, © John Elk/**Tony Stone Images, Inc.;** 34, © John Elk/**Tony Stone Images, Inc.;** 35, © James P. Rowan/**Tony Stone Images, Inc.;** 36, © Buddy Mays/**Travel Stock;** 37 (top), © Greg Vaughn/**Tom Stack & Associates;** 37 (bottom), © David L. Moore/**Photo Resource Hawaii;** 38, © G. Brad Lewis/**Tony Stone Images, Inc.;** 39, © **Tom Till;** 40, **Hawaii State Archives;** 41, © Franco Salmoiraghi/**Photo Resource Hawaii;** 42, © Paul Chesley/**Tony Stone Images, Inc.;** 43, © **Tom Till;** 44, © Ron Dahlquist/**SuperStock;** 45, © Franco Salmoiraghi/**Photo Resource Hawaii;** 46, **Hawaii State Archives;** 47, **Hawaii State Archives;** 48, **Hawaii Medical Library;** 49, **Wide World Photos, Inc.;** 50, **AP/Wide World Photos;** 51, **AP/Wide World Photos;** 52, **AP/Wide World Photos;** 53, **NASA;** 54 (bottom), © Alan Oddie/**Photo Edit;** 54 (top), © Marc Schechter/**Photo Resource Hawaii;** 55, © Jaime Wellner/**Photo Resource Hawaii;** 56 (top), **Courtesy Flag Research Center, Winchester, Massachusetts 01890;** 57 (top), © Kenneth M. Nagata/**Photo Resource Hawaii;** 57 (middle), © T. Dawson/**Photo Resource Hawaii;** 57 (bottom), © Doc White/**Photo Resource Hawaii;** 59, **AP/Wide World Photos;** 60-61, **Tom Dunnington;** back cover, © Jon K. Ogata/**Photo Resource Hawaii**

INDEX

Page numbers in boldface type indicate illustrations.

ABOUT THE AUTHOR

Dennis Brindell Fradin is the author of 150 published children's books. His works for Childrens Press include the Young People's Stories of Our States series, the Disaster! series, and the Thirteen Colonies series. Dennis is married to Judith Bloom Fradin, who taught high-school and college English for many years. She is now Dennis's chief researcher. The Fradins are the parents of two sons, Anthony and Michael, and a daughter, Diana. Dennis graduated from Northwestern University in 1967 with a B.A. in creative writing, and has lived in Evanston, Illinois, since that year.